Welcome, Dear Readers,

An anonymous author who goes by the pseudonym "Soul Saver" welcomes you to this exceptional journey. We are here to touch upon topics that are often overlooked or hidden. Topics that concern each and every one of us, without exception. Through these words, we aim to create a place where every soul, regardless of their experience, can find support, understanding, and hope.

Our book is not about me but about you. About you and the millions of other people around the world who battle with mental and emotional issues every day. It's a book designed to touch your heart, understand your suffering, and help you on your path to a better tomorrow.

In today's world, full of challenges and tensions, mental and emotional issues are becoming increasingly common. There's no need to hide from this fact. It's important that we, as a society, openly discuss this and work together to find solutions.

In the upcoming chapters of this book, we will explore various types of mental and emotional issues. You will understand where they come from, why they are so challenging to overcome, and, most importantly, how you can cope with them. You are not alone in this battle, and we are here to prove that to you.

We also want to assure you that you are not an anonymous suffering soul. You are an extraordinary being deserving of happiness, love, and support. We are here to support you on this journey, so you don't feel alone in all of this.

Reader, you are important to us. Your suffering matters to us. Together, we will go to great lengths to ease your path through it all.

Together, we will save souls.

Chapter 1: What Are Mental and Emotional Issues?

In this first chapter, we will delve into the fundamental question: What exactly are mental and emotional issues?

Every person on this planet experiences moments when their mind and emotions are in turmoil. These challenges are an integral part of the human experience, and they can manifest in various ways. Whether it's the weight of sadness, the grip of anxiety, or the confusion of conflicting thoughts, we all go through these struggles.

Mental and emotional issues encompass a broad spectrum of conditions that affect our psychological and emotional well-being. They can be temporary, arising from specific life events or circumstances, or they can be long-lasting, deeply rooted in our minds and hearts.

Some common mental and emotional issues include depression, anxiety disorders, bipolar disorder, post-traumatic stress disorder (PTSD), eating disorders, and more. Each of these conditions carries its unique challenges, symptoms, and manifestations, making it crucial to understand them individually.

But what truly defines these issues is their impact on our daily lives. They can disrupt our relationships, hinder our ability to work or study, and diminish our overall quality of life. They create invisible battles within us, affecting our thoughts, emotions, and behavior.

It's essential to recognize that experiencing these issues doesn't make you weak or inferior. They are not a reflection of your character, but rather a testament to your resilience and strength in facing adversity. Just as we can fall ill physically, we can also face challenges mentally and emotionally.

Throughout this book, we will explore various mental and emotional issues in detail. We will delve into their causes, symptoms, and the profound impact they can have on our lives. Most importantly, we will guide you on how to navigate through these challenges and find your path to healing and resilience.

Remember, dear reader, you are not alone in this journey. Your pain is shared by countless others around the world. Together, we will shed light on the darkness that often surrounds mental and emotional issues and work towards a brighter, more hopeful future.

Chapter 2: Where Do Psychological and Emotional Problems Come From?

In the previous chapter, we discussed what psychological and emotional problems are exactly. Now, let's take a closer look at where these difficulties that affect our lives come from.

Psychological and emotional problems don't just appear out of thin air. They have their origins and causes, which are diverse and often complex. Understanding these causes can help us better cope with problems and prevent them from worsening.

1Genetics: Inheritance of genes can play a role in predisposition to certain psychological problems. However, this does not mean that if someone in your family has such problems, you will definitely inherit them. Genetics is just one of many factors.

2Environment: The influence of the environment in which we grow up and live is of great importance. Traumatic events, poverty, violence, or family instability can significantly increase the risk of developing psychological problems.

3Stress: Prolonged or excessive stress can lead to psychological problems, including anxiety disorders and depression. The pressure of daily life, work, school, or relationships can be difficult to bear.

4Biological Factors: Some psychological problems can be caused by changes in the brain or the action of neurochemical processes. For example, deficiencies in neurotransmitters can contribute to mood disorders.

5Trauma: Traumatic experiences such as violence, accidents, abuse, or the loss of a loved one can leave a lasting mark on the psyche and lead to the development of psychological problems, including post-traumatic stress disorder (PTSD).

6Social Conditioning: Society, culture, and norms can influence how we deal with emotions and react to stressful situations. Sometimes these conditioning factors can lead to internalizing problems.

7Lack of Care or Support: Lack of social support, understanding, and assistance can make emotional problems more challenging to overcome.

It is worth noting that every individual is different, and the causes of their problems may be unique. It is not always easy to determine a single cause. The key to effectively addressing psychological and emotional problems is to consult with a professional who can help understand their sources and find appropriate coping strategies.

Chapter 3: Why Is Dealing with Mental and Emotional Issues So Difficult?

In the previous chapters, we discussed what mental and emotional issues are and where they come from. Now it's time to understand why dealing with them can be so challenging. Coping with these issues can be a significant challenge, and understanding the obstacles we face can help us better manage them.

Stigma: One of the main reasons it's challenging to deal with mental and emotional problems is stigma. People often fear openly discussing their issues because of the fear of judgment or rejection by society. This can lead to hiding their difficulties and a lack of support.

1. **Lack of Self-Awareness:** Some people may not recognize or understand their mental or emotional problems. This can lead to unconsciously ignoring them or attempting to cope without proper assistance.

2. **Complexity of Issues:** Mental and emotional problems are often complex and multifaceted. Identifying their causes and effects can be difficult, making it challenging to find suitable solutions.

3. **Negative Impact on Daily Life:** Mental and emotional issues can significantly affect daily life, including work, relationships, and physical health. This can lead to a downward spiral in well-being.

4. **Lack of Access to Help:** Unfortunately, not everyone has easy access to professional psychological help. Long waiting times for consultations or a lack of financial resources for therapy can be obstacles.

5. **Behavioral Changes:** People with mental or emotional

problems often change their behavior in response to their difficulties. This can lead to problems in their relationships with others, further complicating coping.

6 **Lack of Social Support:** Support from family, friends, and the community is invaluable in coping with emotional issues. The absence of this form of support can make the struggle more burdensome.

Despite these challenges, it's important to remember that there is hope. Professional psychological help, therapy, social support, and self-awareness can significantly aid in dealing with mental and emotional problems. In the upcoming chapters, we will discuss various strategies and tools that can be useful in this battle.

Chapter 4: Depression - The Emotional Burden

Introduction

Depression is one of the most common and debilitating emotional disorders that people around the world struggle with. In this chapter, we will take a closer look at this challenging subject, starting with a brief definition of depression and understanding its significance in the context of this book.

What Is Depression?

Depression is a comprehensive emotional disorder that manifests on both a psychological and physical level. Many people tend to confuse depression with ordinary sadness, but they are two different things. In this chapter, we will discuss the symptoms of depression and explain the differences between it and sadness.

Symptoms of depression:

Depression manifests with various symptoms, both psychological and physical. Some of the main symptoms include:

- **Mood Apathy**: Loss of interest and pleasure in everyday activities.

- **Low Self-Worth**: A sense of worthlessness and guilt.
- **Changes in Weight and Appetite**: Weight gain or loss associated with changes in appetite.
- **Sleep Disturbances**: Trouble falling asleep or excessive sleeping.
- **Fatigue**: Difficulty concentrating and lack of energy.
- **Suicidal Thoughts**: Thoughts of self-harm or suicide.

Differences between sadness and depression:

There are key differences between sadness and depression. Sadness is a normal reaction to difficult life situations, such as loss or separation. It is temporary and typically passes after a certain period of time. Depression, on the other hand, is a chronic state that persists for an extended period, often without an obvious reason.

Here is Chapter 4 dedicated to depression:

Chapter 4: Depression - The Emotional Burden

Introduction

Depression is one of the most common and debilitating emotional disorders that people around the world struggle with. In this chapter, we will take a closer look at this challenging subject, starting with a brief definition of depression and understanding its significance in the context of this book.

What Is Depression?

Depression is a comprehensive emotional disorder that manifests on both a psychological and physical level. Many people tend to confuse depression with ordinary sadness, but they are two different things. In this chapter, we will discuss the symptoms of depression and explain the differences between it and sadness.

Symptoms of depression:

Depression manifests with various symptoms, both psychological and physical. Some of the main symptoms include:

- **Mood Apathy**: Loss of interest and pleasure in everyday activities.
- **Low Self-Worth**: A sense of worthlessness and guilt.
- **Changes in Weight and Appetite**: Weight gain or loss associated with changes in appetite.
- **Sleep Disturbances**: Trouble falling asleep or excessive sleeping.
- **Fatigue**: Difficulty concentrating and lack of energy.
- **Suicidal Thoughts**: Thoughts of self-harm or suicide.

Differences between sadness and depression:

There are key differences between sadness and depression. Sadness is a normal reaction to difficult life situations, such as loss or separation. It is temporary and typically passes after a certain period of time. Depression, on the other hand, is a chronic state that persists for an extended period, often without an obvious reason.

Causes of Depression

Depression can have various causes and often results from a combination of factors. Below, we will discuss some of the main causes of depression.

Genetic and Environmental Factors

Research suggests that there is a genetic component to depression. If there have been cases of depression in your family, you may have a higher risk of developing it as well. However, genetics is not the only factor influencing depression.

The environment also plays a significant role. Exposure to stress, trauma, loss, or adverse family conditions can increase the risk of depression.

Recognizing and Diagnosing Depression

Diagnosing depression can be challenging because its symptoms may resemble those of other mental disorders. However, there are steps you can take to identify and diagnose depression.

When to Pay Attention to Symptoms

You should pay attention to depressive symptoms if they persist for at least two weeks and significantly impact your daily functioning. If you find it challenging to carry out regular tasks, such as getting up in the morning, maintaining concentration at work, or experiencing a loss of interest in life, it is advisable to consult with a healthcare professional.

Steps to Diagnosis

The process of diagnosing depression typically involves consulting a doctor or mental health specialist. They will conduct an interview and assess the symptoms, paying attention to their duration and severity. In some cases, tests may be required to rule out other medical conditions that could be causing similar symptoms.

Summary

Depression is a severe emotional disorder affecting many people worldwide. Understanding its nature, symptoms, and causes is essential to effectively combat it. In the following chapters of this book, we will discuss therapies, medications, and strategies that can help individuals suffering from depression, as well as how to cope with this challenging experience.

Chapter 5: Anxiety and Anxiety Disorders - The Battle Within

Introduction

Anxiety is a common and often distressing emotional state experienced by people worldwide. In this chapter, we will delve into the complex world of anxiety and anxiety disorders, starting with a brief definition and exploring their significance in this book.

What Is Anxiety?

Anxiety is a multifaceted emotional state characterized by excessive worry, fear, and apprehension. It can manifest both psychologically and physically, affecting a person's overall well-being. In this chapter, we will outline the symptoms of anxiety and differentiate between everyday worry and anxiety disorders.

Symptoms of anxiety:

Anxiety presents a wide range of symptoms, encompassing both psychological and physical manifestations. Some of the key symptoms include:

Excessive Worry: Persistent and overwhelming concerns about various aspects of life.

- **Restlessness**: An inability to relax or sit still due to heightened inner tension.
- **Physical Symptoms**: Racing heart, muscle tension, sweating, and trembling.
- **Avoidance Behavior**: Avoiding situations or places that trigger anxiety.
- **Irrational Fears**: Experiencing irrational and intense fears or phobias.

Distinguishing everyday worry from anxiety disorders:

While everyone experiences worry from time to time, anxiety disorders involve persistent, excessive, and often irrational fears or worries that interfere with daily life. In this chapter, we will explore the distinctions between typical concerns and clinical anxiety.

Causes of Anxiety

Anxiety disorders can arise from various causes, often involving a combination of factors. Below, we will delve into some of the primary contributors to anxiety.

Genetic and Environmental Factors

Research suggests that genetics can play a role in the development of anxiety disorders. If there is a family history of anxiety or related mental health conditions, you may have a heightened risk.

Environmental factors such as traumatic experiences, chronic stress, or a history of physical or emotional abuse can also contribute to the development of anxiety disorders.

Recognizing and Diagnosing Anxiety Disorders

Identifying and diagnosing anxiety disorders can be intricate due to their overlapping symptoms with other mental health conditions. However, there are steps you can take to recognize and seek professional help.

When to Be Concerned

It's crucial to take note of anxiety symptoms if they persist for a prolonged period and significantly impair your daily functioning. If your anxiety interferes with your work, relationships, or general quality of life, it's advisable to seek assistance from a healthcare professional.

Diagnostic Procedures

Diagnosing anxiety disorders typically involves consultation with a mental health specialist. They will conduct a comprehensive evaluation, considering the duration and severity of your symptoms. In some instances, psychological assessments or questionnaires may be employed to aid in diagnosis.

Summary

Anxiety and anxiety disorders are prevalent and can be highly distressing. Understanding the nature, symptoms, and causes of anxiety is essential for effectively addressing this emotional struggle. In the following chapters of this book, we will explore therapies, treatments, and coping strategies that can assist individuals dealing with anxiety and anxiety disorders, as well as ways to combat the stigma associated with these conditions.

Chapter 6: Eating Disorders - Unraveling the Complex Relationship with Food

Introduction

Eating disorders are complex mental health conditions that revolve around an individual's relationship with food, body image, and self-esteem. In this chapter, we will explore the intricate world of eating disorders, starting with a brief definition and their significance within the context of this book.

What Are Eating Disorders?

Eating disorders encompass a range of conditions characterized by abnormal eating habits, negative body image, and obsessive thoughts related to food and weight. In this chapter, we will delve into the various types of eating disorders, their symptoms, and the critical role they play in mental health.

Common types of eating disorders:

1. **Anorexia Nervosa**: Characterized by extreme calorie restriction, fear of weight gain, and distorted body image.

2. **Bulimia Nervosa**: Involves episodes of binge eating followed by compensatory behaviors such as vomiting or excessive exercise.

3 **Binge-Eating Disorder**: Frequent episodes of overeating without compensatory behaviors, often leading to obesity.

4 **Avoidant/Restrictive Food Intake Disorder (ARFID)**: Selective eating based on food textures, smells, or other sensory issues.

Symptoms and Consequences

Eating disorders come with a host of physical and psychological symptoms that can be detrimental to one's health and overall well-being. Understanding these symptoms is crucial for early detection and intervention.

Common symptoms of eating disorders:

- **Rapid Weight Changes**: Significant fluctuations in body weight, either up or down.
- **Obsession with Food and Calories**: Constant preoccupation with food, diets, and calorie counting.
- **Body Image Distortion**: A distorted perception of one's body size and shape.
- **Physical Health Complications**: Including cardiovascular issues, electrolyte imbalances, and digestive problems.
- **Mental Health Impact**: Anxiety, depression, and social isolation often accompany eating disorders.

Root Causes of Eating Disorders

Understanding the underlying factors that contribute to the development of eating disorders is crucial for effective treatment and support.

Psychosocial Factors

Eating disorders can often be linked to psychosocial factors, such as low self-esteem, perfectionism, or a history of trauma or abuse. We will explore how these factors contribute to the development of eating disorders.

Societal Pressures and Media Influence

The portrayal of unrealistic body standards in media and societal pressures to conform to these standards can play a significant role in the development of eating disorders. We will examine how these external influences affect individuals.

Identifying and Seeking Help

Recognizing the signs of eating disorders in oneself or others is the first step toward seeking help and support.

When to Seek Help

It's crucial to seek professional assistance if you or someone you know is exhibiting symptoms of an eating disorder. Early intervention can improve outcomes and prevent further physical and emotional damage.

Diagnosis and Treatment

Diagnosing and treating eating disorders require a multidisciplinary approach involving medical, nutritional, and psychological assessments. We will discuss the steps involved in diagnosis and the various treatment options available, such as therapy, nutritional counseling, and support groups.

Summary

Eating disorders are intricate conditions that affect individuals physically and emotionally. Understanding the different types, symptoms, root causes, and the process of seeking help is vital for addressing these disorders effectively. In the subsequent chapters of this book, we will delve into therapies, strategies, and resources for individuals struggling with eating disorders and examine ways to reduce the stigma surrounding these conditions.

Chapter 7: Bipolar Disorder - Navigating the Peaks and Valleys of Emotions

Introduction

Bipolar disorder is a mental health condition characterized by extreme mood swings, encompassing both manic and depressive episodes. In this chapter, we will explore the complexities of bipolar disorder, starting with a brief definition and its significance within the context of this book.

What Is Bipolar Disorder?

Bipolar disorder, often referred to as manic-depressive illness, is marked by intense and fluctuating mood changes. Individuals with bipolar disorder experience periods of elevated energy and euphoria (mania) followed by periods of extreme sadness and hopelessness (depression).

Common Types of Bipolar Disorder:

1. **Bipolar I Disorder**: Characterized by manic episodes that last at least seven days or are severe enough to require immediate hospitalization, often followed by depressive episodes.

2. **Bipolar II Disorder**: Characterized by hypomanic episodes (less severe than full mania) and depressive episodes.

3. **Cyclothymic Disorder**: Involves periods of hypomanic symptoms and mild depression for at least two years (or one year in children and adolescents).

Symptoms and Impact

Bipolar disorder presents a range of symptoms and can significantly affect an individual's life. Understanding these symptoms is crucial for early diagnosis and effective management.

Common symptoms of bipolar disorder:

- **Manic Symptoms**: Increased energy, racing thoughts, impulsivity, and decreased need for sleep.
- **Depressive Symptoms**: Persistent sadness, loss of interest, changes in appetite and sleep, and feelings of worthlessness.
- **Cognitive and Behavioral Changes**: Impaired decision-making during manic episodes and difficulty concentrating during depressive episodes.

Root Causes of Bipolar Disorder

The exact cause of bipolar disorder is not yet fully understood, but research suggests it may be linked to a combination of genetic, biochemical, and environmental factors.

Genetic Factors

A family history of bipolar disorder can increase an individual's risk of developing the condition. We will explore the genetic underpinnings of bipolar disorder and the role of specific genes.

Neurochemical Imbalances

Changes in neurotransmitter levels, particularly in dopamine and serotonin, are associated with bipolar disorder. We will delve into how these imbalances contribute to mood swings.

Environmental Triggers

Stressful life events, substance abuse, and disruptions in circadian rhythms can trigger manic or depressive episodes in individuals with a predisposition to bipolar disorder.

Diagnosis and Treatment

Diagnosing and managing bipolar disorder is essential for improving an individual's quality of life.

The Diagnostic Process

Recognizing the symptoms and seeking help are the initial steps in the diagnostic process. We will discuss the importance of thorough psychiatric evaluations and assessments.

Treatment Approaches

Bipolar disorder often requires a combination of treatments, including medication and therapy. We will explore the various treatment options available and the importance of medication adherence.

Coping and Support

Living with bipolar disorder can be challenging, but with the right strategies and support, individuals can manage their condition effectively.

Self-Care and Coping Strategies

We will provide practical tips and coping strategies for individuals with bipolar disorder to help them navigate the highs and lows of their condition.

Building a Support System

Having a strong support network, including friends and family, is crucial in managing bipolar disorder. We will discuss the significance of a support system and ways to build and maintain it.

Summary

Bipolar disorder is a complex mental health condition characterized by extreme mood swings. Understanding the types, symptoms, root causes, diagnosis, and treatment options for bipolar disorder is essential for individuals living with this condition and their loved ones. In the subsequent chapters of this book, we will delve deeper into coping mechanisms, therapy approaches, and resources available to support those affected by bipolar disorder and work toward reducing the stigma surrounding mental health.

Chapter 8: Personality Disorders - Unraveling the Complexities of the Self

Introduction

Personality disorders represent a group of mental health conditions characterized by enduring patterns of behavior, cognition, and inner experience that significantly deviate from societal expectations. This chapter explores the intricate world of personality disorders, beginning with a brief definition and their significance within the context of this book.

What Are Personality Disorders?

Personality disorders are enduring and inflexible patterns of behavior, cognition, and inner experience that deviate from cultural expectations and lead to distress or impairment. These patterns affect how individuals perceive themselves, relate to others, and navigate the world around them.

Common Types of Personality Disorders:

1. **Borderline Personality Disorder (BPD)**: Marked by instability in relationships, self-image, and emotions, often leading to impulsive behaviors and intense, unstable moods.

2. **Narcissistic Personality Disorder**: Characterized by an inflated sense of self-importance, a lack of empathy, and a constant need for admiration.

3. **Antisocial Personality Disorder (ASPD)**: Involves a disregard for the rights of others, impulsivity, and a lack of remorse for harmful actions.

4. **Obsessive-Compulsive Personality Disorder (OCPD)**: Defined by an excessive preoccupation with rules,

orderliness, and control, often at the expense of flexibility and openness.

Symptoms and Impact

Personality disorders can have a profound impact on an individual's life, affecting their relationships, work, and overall well-being. Recognizing these symptoms is crucial for early diagnosis and effective management.

Common symptoms of personality disorders:

- **Interpersonal Challenges**: Difficulty establishing and maintaining healthy relationships.
- **Emotional Dysregulation**: Intense mood swings and emotional instability.
- **Maladaptive Behaviors**: Engaging in impulsive, self-destructive, or harmful behaviors.
- **Cognitive Distortions**: Distorted thought patterns and beliefs about oneself and others.

Underlying Factors of Personality Disorders

While the precise causes of personality disorders are complex and multifaceted, a combination of genetic, environmental, and psychological factors may contribute to their development.

Genetic and Biological Factors

Research suggests that there may be a genetic predisposition to certain personality disorders, making individuals more susceptible to their development.

Early Life Experiences

Childhood experiences, including trauma, neglect, or inconsistent caregiving, can contribute to the development of personality disorders.

Cognitive and Psychological Factors

Maladaptive thought patterns and cognitive distortions often play a role in the development and perpetuation of personality disorders.

Diagnosis and Treatment

Diagnosing and managing personality disorders require a comprehensive approach that considers both the individual's unique experiences and the specific type of personality disorder.

The Diagnostic Process

Diagnosing personality disorders involves a thorough assessment of the individual's history, behavior, and symptoms. We will explore the importance of accurate diagnosis and its role in guiding treatment.

Treatment Approaches

Treatment for personality disorders often involves psychotherapy, medication, and support. We will discuss the various therapeutic modalities and the potential benefits of each.

Coping and Support

Living with a personality disorder can be challenging, but with appropriate strategies and a strong support system, individuals can lead fulfilling lives.

Self-Care and Coping Strategies

We will provide practical self-care strategies and coping mechanisms to help individuals manage the challenges associated with personality disorders.

Building a Support Network

Developing a reliable support network can be instrumental in the recovery process. We will explore ways to build and maintain a supportive community.

Summary

Personality disorders represent complex challenges that affect how individuals perceive themselves and interact with the world. Understanding the types, symptoms, underlying factors, diagnosis, and treatment options for personality disorders is essential for individuals living with these conditions and their loved ones. In the following chapters of this book, we will delve deeper into coping strategies, therapy approaches, and available resources to support those affected by personality disorders and reduce the stigma surrounding mental health.

Chapter 9: Addictions - Breaking Free from the Chains

Introduction

Addiction is a complex and pervasive issue that affects millions of people worldwide. This chapter explores the nature of addiction, its various forms, and the critical importance of understanding and addressing it.

Understanding Addiction

Addiction refers to the compulsive engagement in a behavior or the use of a substance, despite harmful consequences. It often starts as a voluntary choice but can progress into a deeply ingrained and difficult-to-control pattern.

Common Types of Addictions:

1. **Substance Use Disorders**: Involves addiction to substances like drugs, alcohol, and prescription medications.

2. **Behavioral Addictions**: Includes addictions to activities such as gambling, gaming, shopping, and overeating.

The Vicious Cycle

Addiction operates in a cycle of craving, use, and negative consequences, making it a challenging issue to overcome. This chapter delves into the cycle's components and how they perpetuate addiction.

The Cycle of Addiction:

1. **Craving**: The intense desire or urge to engage in the addictive behavior or consume the substance.

2. **Use**: Acting on the craving by engaging in the behavior or using the substance.

3. **Negative Consequences**: Experiencing detrimental effects on one's physical health, mental well-being, relationships, and overall life.

Risk Factors and Vulnerability

Certain factors can increase an individual's susceptibility to addiction, including genetic predisposition, environmental influences, and mental health conditions.

Breaking Free from Addiction

Overcoming addiction is a challenging journey that requires commitment, support, and effective strategies. This chapter explores the critical steps toward recovery.

Recognizing the Problem

Acknowledging the presence of addiction is the first and often the most challenging step. We discuss the signs and symptoms that can help individuals recognize their addiction.

Seeking Help

Professional help, whether through therapy, counseling, or support groups, plays a pivotal role in recovery. We delve into the different forms of treatment available.

Coping and Relapse Prevention

Developing healthy coping mechanisms and strategies to prevent relapse is vital for maintaining long-term recovery.

Coping Strategies for Recovery:

- **Mindfulness and Stress Reduction**: Techniques for managing stress and cravings.
- **Healthy Lifestyle Choices**: Adopting a balanced and fulfilling lifestyle that supports recovery.
- **Supportive Relationships**: Building and maintaining relationships that encourage sobriety.

The Role of Support

Family, friends, and support groups provide essential support during the recovery process. We explore how to build a robust support network.

Ending the Stigma

Addiction is often accompanied by stigma and misunderstanding. In this chapter, we discuss the importance of destigmatizing addiction and promoting empathy and understanding.

Challenging Misconceptions

We address common misconceptions about addiction and how they can hinder recovery efforts.

Promoting Compassion

By fostering a compassionate and non-judgmental society, we can create a more supportive environment for those struggling with addiction.

Summary

Addiction is a multifaceted issue that affects individuals physically, mentally, and emotionally. Understanding its nature, recognizing the signs, and seeking help are critical steps toward recovery. This chapter provides insights into the various forms of addiction, the cycle that perpetuates it, and the strategies for breaking free. In the following chapters of this book, we will delve deeper into specific addictions, treatment approaches, and the importance of empathy and support in the journey to recovery.

Chapter 10: Mood Disorders - Navigating the Emotional Rollercoaster

Introduction

Mood disorders are a category of mental health conditions that primarily affect an individual's emotional state. This chapter explores the nature of mood disorders, their various types, and strategies for managing them.

Understanding Mood Disorders

Mood disorders are characterized by disturbances in a person's mood, leading to significant distress and impairment in daily functioning. This chapter provides an overview of mood disorders, their prevalence, and their impact on individuals.

Common Types of Mood Disorders:

1. **Major Depressive Disorder (MDD)**: Marked by persistent and severe feelings of sadness and loss of interest or pleasure in most activities.

2. **Bipolar Disorder**: Involves cycling between episodes of depression and mania (elevated mood and heightened energy).

The Emotional Rollercoaster

Living with a mood disorder can feel like riding an emotional rollercoaster. This chapter delves into the ups and downs of these conditions and their impact on individuals' lives.

The Cycle of Mood Disorders:

1 **Depressive Episodes**: Overwhelming sadness, hopelessness, and lack of interest or pleasure.

2 **Manic or Hypomanic Episodes** (in Bipolar Disorder): Elevated mood, increased energy, and impulsivity.

Risk Factors and Triggers

Several factors contribute to the development of mood disorders, including genetic predisposition, brain chemistry, life events, and chronic stress.

Managing Mood Disorders

While mood disorders can be challenging to live with, effective management and support are available. This chapter explores strategies for individuals and their loved ones.

Seeking Professional Help

Professional intervention, such as therapy and medication, plays a crucial role in managing mood disorders. We discuss the various therapeutic approaches and the importance of medication management.

Lifestyle Modifications

Adopting a healthy lifestyle that includes regular exercise, a balanced diet, adequate sleep, and stress management can help stabilize mood.

Coping Strategies

Developing coping mechanisms for dealing with mood swings and emotional challenges is essential. We provide practical techniques for managing symptoms.

Coping Strategies for Mood Disorders:

- **Cognitive Behavioral Therapy (CBT)**: Identifying and changing negative thought patterns.
- **Mindfulness and Meditation**: Techniques for staying present and reducing emotional reactivity.
- **Supportive Relationships**: Building a network of understanding friends and family members.

Self-Care and Relapse Prevention

Preventing relapses and maintaining emotional well-being is a crucial aspect of managing mood disorders.

Ending the Silence

Stigma and misconceptions often surround mood disorders, preventing individuals from seeking help. In this chapter, we discuss the importance of raising awareness and eliminating stigma.

Challenging Myths

We address common myths and misconceptions about mood disorders and their impact on individuals.

Promoting Acceptance and Empathy

Creating a compassionate and empathetic society can help individuals with mood disorders feel understood and supported.

Summary

Mood disorders can significantly affect an individual's emotional well-being and daily life. Understanding the different types of mood disorders, their cycles, and potential triggers is essential. Seeking professional help, adopting a healthy lifestyle, developing coping strategies, and promoting empathy and acceptance are vital steps toward effectively managing these conditions. In the upcoming chapters, we will explore specific mood disorders in more detail, their treatment options, and the importance of community support.

Chapter 11: Effective Coping Strategies for Dealing with Emotional Issues

Section 1: Understanding and Acceptance

Understanding and acceptance are crucial stages in the process of coping with emotional issues. In this section, we will discuss why these aspects are so important and how you can develop them to start your journey towards healing.

Understanding Emotional Issues

Let's start by understanding what emotional issues are. They can include depression, anxiety, eating disorders, bipolar disorder, personality disorders, addictions, and many more. The most important thing is that they are real and often challenging experiences that impact our daily lives.

Understanding Your Emotions

The first step in coping with emotional issues is understanding your emotions. This means being aware of your feelings and thoughts. Often, individuals with emotional issues experience complex emotions that may be difficult to name. Understanding what is happening within you can help identify the problem and initiate the healing process.

Acceptance

Acceptance is a crucial element in coping with emotional issues. It means accepting that you are affected by an emotional problem and understanding that it is not your fault. Emotional issues can affect anyone, regardless of age, gender, or social status. Accepting your situation is important because it allows you to start working on it.

The Value of Self-awareness

Self-awareness, or the ability to recognize your feelings, thoughts, and needs, is a key aspect of coping with emotional issues. Recognizing your emotions enables you to take conscious actions towards resolving them. It also helps avoid communication breakdowns with others, which can be particularly important in terms of social support.

The Role of Therapy in Understanding and Acceptance

Psychological therapy, especially cognitive-behavioral therapy (CBT), can be incredibly helpful in understanding and accepting emotional issues. Therapists assist patients in identifying negative thoughts and beliefs that may contribute to emotional problems and help them develop healthier thinking patterns.

Summary

Understanding and accepting your emotional issues are crucial stages in coping with them. It marks the beginning of your journey towards healing, enabling you to cope more effectively with difficulties and opening doors to various forms of support. Remember that you are not alone in your struggle, and there are professionals and loved ones who want to help you on this journey.

Chapter 12: Self-Help and Education as Key Tools in Dealing with Emotional Issues

Section 1: Self-Help - Strength Lies Within You

Self-help is an incredibly powerful tool in coping with emotional issues. In this section, we will discuss why it's worth developing and what benefits can be gained from it.

Self-Help - What Is It?

Let's start by understanding what self-help is. It's a process in which we take steps on our own to improve our mental and emotional well-being. Self-help involves actions taken independently to address emotional problems and strive for greater well-being.

Benefits of Self-Help

Self-help offers many benefits. Firstly, it gives us a sense of control over our lives and the healing process. It enables us to act independently, regardless of external factors. Self-help teaches us how to deal with difficulties, which can bring long-term advantages.

Different Forms of Self-Help

Self-help can take many forms. It can be journaling, practicing yoga, meditation, or learning new skills. The key is to find an approach that suits your needs and lifestyle.

Education About Emotional Issues

Another crucial element in coping with emotional problems is education. Understanding the mechanisms at play in your body and mind during tough times can help you handle them better.

Benefits of Education

Gaining knowledge about your emotional state and possible issues is the first step toward effectively coping with them. Education helps you understand why certain symptoms occur and what treatment and support options are available.

Educational Therapy

Educational therapy is an effective tool that helps patients understand and manage their emotional problems. Therapists guide patients in the process of learning about their emotions and provide them with tools to cope with them.

Summary

Self-help and education are key tools that help in dealing with emotional issues. They empower you to take control of your mental health and provide you with the knowledge necessary for effective management of emotional difficulties. Don't hesitate to use these tools—they are available to you and can significantly improve your well-being and quality of life.

Chapter 13: Social Support - A Source of Hope

Section 1: Social Support - What Is It?

Social support is one of the most crucial factors affecting our mental and emotional well-being. In this section, we will discuss in detail what social support is and why it is so significant.

Social Support - Definition

Social support refers to the assistance and help we receive from our social environment, which includes family, friends, life partners, and other important people in our lives. This support can take various forms, including emotional, instrumental (practical), and informational.

The Role of Social Support in Our Lives

Social support forms the foundation of our mental well-being. It helps us cope with difficulties, reduce stress, and adapt better to life changes. It is crucial both in preventing emotional problems and in the healing process.

Forms of Social Support

Social support can come in various forms. It can be emotional support, which includes support through listening, understanding, and expressing empathy. Instrumental support involves practical help, such as assistance with daily tasks or financial support. Informational support provides information and guidance on how to deal with a problem.

Building and Maintaining Social Support

Investing time and effort in building and maintaining social support is worthwhile. It is not only beneficial in difficult times but also enhances our overall psychological resilience. Establishing lasting relationships based on mutual support is crucial.

Social Support and Mental Health

Research shows that individuals with strong social support are less vulnerable to emotional issues such as depression and anxiety. Additionally, they have a better chance of improving their mental health if they are already experiencing such problems.

Summary

Social support is the cornerstone of our mental health. Understanding its importance and actively building relationships based on mutual support can significantly impact the quality of our lives and our ability to cope with emotional difficulties. Do not hesitate to seek support from your social environment and offer it to others when they are in need. It is an investment in our mental well-being that yields numerous benefits.

Chapter 14: A Healthy Lifestyle - Your Path to Wellness

Section 1: A Healthy Lifestyle - What Is It?

In this section, we will delve into the concept of a healthy lifestyle, its components, and its profound impact on your overall well-being.

A Healthy Lifestyle - Definition

A healthy lifestyle is a way of living that promotes physical, mental, and emotional well-being. It involves adopting habits and behaviors that contribute to your overall health and longevity.

The Components of a Healthy Lifestyle

A healthy lifestyle comprises various essential components, including:

1. **Nutrition**: Eating a balanced diet that provides essential nutrients, vitamins, and minerals for optimal bodily function.

2. **Physical Activity**: Regular exercise and physical activity are crucial for maintaining a healthy body, reducing the risk of chronic diseases, and improving mental health.

3. **Sleep**: Getting adequate and quality sleep is vital for physical and mental recovery and overall well-being.

4. **Stress Management**: Effectively managing stress through relaxation techniques, mindfulness, or meditation can greatly impact your emotional health.

5. **Substance Avoidance**: Avoiding harmful substances such as tobacco, excessive alcohol, and illicit drugs is essential for a healthy lifestyle.

6. **Hydration**: Staying well-hydrated is crucial for bodily

functions, and it impacts energy levels and mental clarity.

7 **Mental and Emotional Health**: Nurturing your mental and emotional well-being through self-care, seeking support when needed, and practicing resilience is a core component of a healthy lifestyle.

Benefits of a Healthy Lifestyle

Embracing a healthy lifestyle offers numerous benefits, including:

- **Improved Physical Health**: Reduced risk of chronic diseases, better immune function, and increased longevity.

- **Enhanced Mental Health**: Improved mood, reduced risk of mental health issues, and better stress management.

- **Increased Energy**: A well-balanced lifestyle results in higher energy levels and increased productivity.

- **Better Quality of Life**: A healthy lifestyle contributes to an overall improved quality of life, increased happiness, and greater life satisfaction.

Incorporating a Healthy Lifestyle

It's essential to understand that adopting a healthy lifestyle is a gradual process. Start by setting realistic goals, making small changes, and seeking support from healthcare professionals or support groups when necessary.

Summary

A healthy lifestyle is not a destination but a continuous journey toward improved physical, mental, and emotional well-being. It involves various components that, when combined, contribute to a happier, healthier, and more fulfilling life. Remember that every positive change you make in your lifestyle can have a significant impact on your overall wellness.

Chapter 15: The Role of Therapy in Understanding and Acceptance

Section 1: Therapy as the Key to Understanding

In this chapter, we will delve into the primary role of therapy in the process of understanding and accepting one's own psychological and emotional problems. Therapy plays an irreplaceable role in helping individuals explore their thoughts, feelings, and experiences in a safe and supportive environment. Through regular therapeutic sessions, the patient gains the opportunity for self-discovery. The therapist assists in identifying hidden thought patterns, beliefs, and defense mechanisms that may affect one's well-being and behavior.

Therapy and Self-Awareness

Therapy provides a safe and supportive environment in which a patient can delve into their thoughts, emotions, and experiences. Through regular therapeutic sessions, a patient gains the opportunity for self-discovery. The therapist helps in identifying hidden thought patterns, beliefs, and defense mechanisms that may affect one's well-being and behavior.

Understanding the Causes

Therapy helps the patient understand the causes of their emotional and psychological problems. Often, these causes are complex and stem from the past, trauma, or childhood experiences. Therapy enables the patient to identify how these causes have impacted their current life and behavior.

Section 2: Therapy and Acceptance

Acceptance of Oneself and One's Problems

Therapy supports the process of accepting oneself and one's problems. People grappling with psychological or emotional issues often experience shame, guilt, or self-criticism. The therapist helps the patient understand that these feelings are normal and that they are not to blame for their problems.

Combatting Stigmatization

Therapy assists in combatting the stigma associated with emotional problems. The therapist can provide the patient with tools to cope with negative stereotypes and societal biases against individuals with emotional issues.

Section 3: Therapy as a Path to Healthy Functioning

Developing Coping Skills

Therapy allows the patient to develop coping skills for emotional and psychological difficulties. The therapist provides tools and strategies to help shift destructive thought patterns and behaviors towards healthier ones.

Support in the Healing Process

The therapist offers emotional support, which is crucial in the healing process. The patient knows that they are not alone and has someone with whom they can share their most challenging feelings and thoughts.

Summary: Therapy as a Critical Part of Your Mental Health Journey

Therapy is an invaluable tool in the process of understanding and accepting one's psychological and emotional problems. It is a space where individuals can work on change and personal growth. Together with a therapist, patients can find balance and improved well-being, which is a critical part of the journey to mental health.

Chapter 16: The Importance of Self-Care

Section 1: What is Self-Care?

In this chapter, we will explore the concept of self-care and its significance in maintaining good mental and emotional health. Self-care encompasses a range of activities and practices that are deliberately undertaken to promote overall well-being. It is about taking the time to nurture yourself physically, emotionally, and mentally.

The Elements of Self-Care

Self-care involves various elements, including physical health, emotional well-being, and psychological balance. It encompasses practices like maintaining a balanced diet, engaging in regular exercise, getting enough sleep, and managing stress effectively.

Section 2: The Significance of Self-Care

Self-Care as a Necessity, Not a Luxury

Self-care is not a luxury but a necessity. It is essential for everyone, regardless of their age, gender, or life circumstances. Engaging in self-care activities helps prevent burnout, reduce stress, and improve overall quality of life.

The Relationship Between Self-Care and Mental Health

There is a strong connection between self-care and mental health. Neglecting self-care can contribute to the development or exacerbation of mental health issues. Conversely, practicing self-care can be an effective way to manage and prevent mental health problems.

Section 3: Incorporating Self-Care Into Your Life

Identifying Your Self-Care Needs

Each individual's self-care needs are unique. It is crucial to identify what activities and practices make you feel most rejuvenated and at peace. Self-awareness is a key component of effective self-care.

Building Self-Care Habits

Incorporating self-care into your daily routine involves building healthy habits. This can include setting aside time for relaxation, engaging in hobbies you enjoy, and seeking support from friends and family when needed.

Summary: Prioritizing Self-Care for Better Mental and Emotional Well-Being

Self-care is an essential aspect of maintaining good mental and emotional health. By understanding the concept of self-care, recognizing its significance, and incorporating self-care practices into your daily life, you can take proactive steps to nurture your well-being and lead a more balanced and fulfilling life.

Chapter 18: Mental Health vs. Physical Health

Mental health and physical health are intimately interconnected. While they may appear as separate spheres, they significantly influence each other. In this chapter, you will learn about the relationships between mental and physical health and why taking care of both aspects is crucial for overall well-being.

The Importance of Balance Between Mental and Physical Health

- Mental health plays a vital role in the quality of life. It is a state of emotional and psychological well-being that allows us to cope with daily challenges.
- Physical health encompasses the condition of the body, organ function, energy levels, and the ability to perform daily activities.

The Impact of Mental Health on Physical Health

- Research indicates that stress, depression, and other emotional issues can negatively affect physical health, increasing the risk of heart disease, hypertension, obesity, and other conditions.
- Mental health influences our dietary habits, physical activity, and sleep, all of which have a profound impact on our overall well-being.

The Impact of Physical Health on Mental Health

- Regular physical activity, such as walking, yoga, or swimming, can help reduce stress and improve mood by releasing endorphins, the "feel-good" hormones.
- A diet rich in vegetables, fruits, whole grains, fish, and healthy fats supports the health of both the body and mind.

Practical Ways to Maintain Balance

- Engage in regular physical activity, such as walking, yoga, or swimming, to maintain both mental and physical health.
- Adopt a diet rich in vegetables, fruits, whole grains, fish, and healthy fats to support overall well-being.
- Practice relaxation techniques like meditation and deep breathing to reduce stress and enhance mental health.
- Ensure adequate sleep as sleep deprivation can negatively affect emotional regulation.

Conclusion

Understanding the connection between mental and physical health is essential for achieving overall well-being. By taking care of both aspects, we can improve our quality of life, reduce the risk of various diseases, and enhance our ability to cope with daily challenges.

Remember that what you do for your mental health has an impact on your physical health and vice versa. Take a comprehensive approach to self-care to achieve full health and harmony.

Chapter 19: Developing Coping Skills

Coping skills are the tools we use to manage stress, deal with challenges, and navigate life's ups and downs effectively. In this chapter, we will explore the importance of developing coping skills and provide practical guidance on honing these essential abilities.

Understanding Coping Skills

- Coping skills encompass a range of strategies and techniques that help individuals adapt to difficult situations and emotions.
- These skills are not one-size-fits-all; they vary from person to person and can be learned and improved upon over time.

The Significance of Effective Coping Skills

- Effective coping skills enhance our resilience, enabling us to bounce back from setbacks and face adversity with confidence.
- They contribute to better mental and emotional well-being, helping to reduce symptoms of anxiety and depression.

Types of Coping Skills

- Problem-solving coping skills involve identifying challenges and finding practical solutions to address them.
- Emotion-focused coping skills emphasize managing emotional responses to stress, such as relaxation techniques or mindfulness meditation.

Developing Coping Skills

- Self-awareness is the first step in developing coping skills. Understanding your unique stressors and emotional triggers is crucial.
- Practice is key. Regularly engage in coping strategies that resonate with you to reinforce these skills.
- Seek professional guidance or therapy if you find it challenging to develop effective coping skills independently.

Specific Coping Techniques

- Mindfulness and meditation practices can help you stay grounded in the present moment and reduce stress and anxiety.
- Deep breathing exercises are simple yet powerful techniques that can calm your nervous system and ease tension.
- Journaling can provide a healthy outlet for expressing emotions and gaining clarity on your thoughts and feelings.

Building Resilience

- Resilience is the ability to adapt and bounce back from adversity. Developing coping skills is an essential component of resilience.
- Cultivate a growth mindset, which encourages you to view challenges as opportunities for growth and learning.

Conclusion

Developing coping skills is an ongoing process that can significantly improve your ability to navigate life's challenges. By understanding different types of coping strategies and practicing them regularly, you can enhance your emotional resilience and overall well-being. Remember that it's okay to seek help and support from mental health professionals when needed. Building effective coping skills is an investment in your mental and emotional health that pays off in countless ways.

Chapter 20: Mindfulness and Meditation – The Path to Mental Health

Mindfulness and meditation are practices that can significantly impact your mental health. In this chapter, we will explore why they are so important and how you can start using them to improve your well-being and emotional balance.

Mindfulness – Awareness of the Present Moment

- Mindfulness, also known as awareness, involves being aware of the present moment. It is a practice that teaches you to observe your thoughts, emotions, and body without judgment.
- Practicing mindfulness helps reduce the impact of stress on your life, improves concentration, and assists in dealing with difficult emotions.

Benefits of Practicing Mindfulness

- Stress and anxiety reduction: Mindfulness helps recognize and control negative thoughts and reactions to stressful situations.
- Improved mental health: Regular mindfulness practice can reduce symptoms of depression and enhance overall well-being.
- Enhanced focus: Mindfulness can improve concentration and the ability to perform tasks.
- Increased self-awareness: Through mindfulness, you become more aware of your emotions, which can help in better emotional management.

Meditation – Tranquil Practice for the Mind

- Meditation is a practice of focusing on one point, thought, or feeling. It can take various forms such as breath meditation, transcendental meditation, or mindfulness meditation.
- Meditation helps achieve peace of mind, reduce stress, and increase internal balance.

Getting Started with Mindfulness and Meditation

- Choose the right place: Find a quiet and peaceful place where you can concentrate.
- Begin with your breath: In breath meditation, focus on your breath, concentrating on its rhythm and depth.

- Patience: Mindfulness and meditation are skills that require practice. Don't get discouraged if it's challenging to concentrate at the beginning.

Integrating Mindfulness and Meditation into Daily Life

- Practicing mindfulness and meditation doesn't have to be limited to silent sessions. You can integrate these techniques into your daily life by practicing them during various activities.

- This provides benefits both at work and in your personal life, helping you maintain composure and emotional balance even in challenging situations.

Summary

Mindfulness and meditation are effective tools for supporting mental health. Regular practice can help reduce stress, improve well-being, enhance concentration, and increase self-awareness. Start with small steps and allow yourself to reap the benefits of these practices that positively impact your life.

Chapter 21: Self-Esteem and Positive Thinking – Building a Strong Foundation

In this chapter, we will delve into the crucial aspects of self-esteem and positive thinking. These elements form a solid foundation for maintaining good mental health and fostering resilience in the face of life's challenges.

Understanding Self-Esteem

- Self-esteem refers to the value and worth you attribute to yourself. It encompasses your overall self-perception and self-acceptance.

- Healthy self-esteem is essential for emotional well-being and plays a vital role in how you perceive and interact with the world.

Signs of Healthy Self-Esteem

- Confidence: Believing in your abilities and feeling confident in your decisions.
- Self-acceptance: Embracing your strengths and weaknesses without harsh self-criticism.
- Resilience: Bouncing back from setbacks and failures with a positive attitude.

Factors Influencing Self-Esteem

- Early life experiences: Childhood experiences, upbringing, and parental influences can significantly impact self-esteem.
- Self-talk: The way you speak to yourself internally can either bolster or undermine your self-esteem.
- Achievements and failures: Successes can boost self-esteem, while failures can challenge it.

Fostering Positive Thinking

- Positive thinking involves focusing on constructive and optimistic perspectives in various situations.
- It can lead to increased overall life satisfaction and improved mental health.

Practical Steps for Cultivating Positive Thinking

- Self-awareness: Pay attention to your thoughts and recognize negative or self-critical patterns.
- Reframe negative thoughts: Challenge and reframe negative thoughts into more positive and realistic ones.
- Gratitude practice: Regularly acknowledge and appreciate the positive aspects of your life.
- Surround yourself with positivity: Spend time with people who uplift and support you.

The Connection Between Self-Esteem and Positive Thinking

- Healthy self-esteem lays the groundwork for cultivating positive thinking. When you feel good about yourself, it becomes easier to adopt a positive outlook on life.
- Positive thinking, in turn, can bolster self-esteem by fostering a more nurturing and affirming inner dialogue.

Summary

In this chapter, we explored the essential concepts of self-esteem and positive thinking. Developing healthy self-esteem and adopting positive thinking patterns are key components of maintaining good mental health and emotional resilience. By recognizing and challenging negative thought patterns and embracing self-acceptance, you can build a strong foundation for emotional well-being and personal growth.

Chapter 22: Managing Difficult Emotions – Navigating the Storm

In this chapter, we will delve into the art of managing challenging emotions. Emotions are a natural part of the human experience, and understanding how to navigate them is essential for maintaining emotional well-being and mental health.

Understanding Emotions

- Emotions are complex and multifaceted responses to various situations and stimuli.
- They encompass a wide range of feelings, from joy and love to anger and sadness.

The Role of Emotions

- Emotions serve as signals that provide valuable information about our inner experiences and external surroundings.
- They can motivate action, deepen relationships, and offer insight into our needs and desires.

Common Challenging Emotions

- Anger: An emotional response to perceived threats, frustration, or injustice.
- Sadness: A natural reaction to loss, disappointment, or adversity.
- Anxiety: A feeling of unease or worry, often about future events or uncertainties.
- Fear: An emotional response to immediate danger or perceived threats.

Healthy Ways to Manage Difficult Emotions

- Self-awareness: Recognize and acknowledge your emotions without judgment.
- Mindfulness: Practice staying present in the moment and observing your emotions without reacting impulsively.
- Emotional expression: Find healthy outlets for your emotions, such as talking to a friend or journaling.
- Relaxation techniques: Engage in relaxation exercises like deep breathing or meditation to calm the nervous system.

Developing Emotional Resilience

- Emotional resilience involves the ability to bounce back from adversity and adapt to life's challenges.
- It can be cultivated through self-care, social support, and emotional regulation strategies.

The Connection Between Emotions and Mental Health

- Unmanaged or suppressed emotions can contribute to mental health issues such as depression, anxiety, or even physical health problems.
- Learning to manage emotions effectively is essential for overall well-being.

Summary

In this chapter, we explored the nature of emotions and their role in our lives. We discussed common challenging emotions and provided strategies for managing them in healthy ways. Developing emotional resilience and recognizing the connection between emotions and mental health are crucial steps in maintaining emotional well-being. By embracing our emotions and learning to navigate them, we can lead more fulfilling and balanced lives.

Chapter 23: The Role of Interpersonal Relationships - Building Support

In this chapter, we will discuss the crucial role of interpersonal relationships in maintaining mental and emotional well-being. Our connections with other people play a significant role in shaping our sense of well-being and how we cope with life's challenges.

The Significance of Relationships

- Interpersonal relationships provide emotional and social support that is essential for our well-being.
- They create a sense of belonging and acceptance, positively impacting our self-esteem.

Social Support

- Social support includes emotional, practical, and informational assistance from other people.
- It can involve conversations with friends, family support, or participation in support groups.

Building and Maintaining Healthy Relationships

- Communication: Open, honest, and empathetic communication is crucial for healthy relationships.
- Empathy: The ability to understand and empathize with the emotions of others is the foundation of strong bonds.
- Shared Activities: Spending time together and engaging in shared activities strengthens bonds.

Negative Relationships and Their Impact

- Toxic relationships can have a detrimental impact on mental health.
- Consider limiting contact with individuals who cause stress

or toxic emotions.

Support in Difficult Times

- It's important to remember that relationships can provide support during challenging periods in life, such as illness, loss, or emotional difficulties.
- Sharing one's hardships with loved ones can make it easier to weather crises.

The Importance of Healthy Boundaries

- Establishing healthy boundaries in relationships is essential for maintaining balance and avoiding emotional overload.

Summary

In this chapter, we explored the significance of interpersonal relationships for mental and emotional well-being. We shared tips on building and maintaining healthy relationships and discussed the impact of negative relationships. We also learned how relationships can provide support during challenging times. Understanding the role of interpersonal relationships can help us build more satisfying and supportive lives.

Chapter 24: Specialist Support - Seeking Help from Professionals

In this chapter, we will discuss the importance of specialist support for individuals dealing with mental and emotional issues. Professional help can be a crucial part of the healing process and coping with difficulties.

The Value of Professionals' Help

- Professionals such as psychotherapists, psychiatrists, or psychologists possess specialized knowledge and tools to assist in resolving emotional problems.
- Seeking help from professionals is a testament to courage and determination in dealing with difficulties.

Psychotherapy

- Therapy can be an effective form of assistance in resolving emotional problems.
- Various therapeutic approaches are available, such as cognitive-behavioral therapy, mindfulness-based cognitive therapy, or psychodynamic psychotherapy.

Antidepressant Medication and Medications

- In some cases, antidepressant medications or other drugs may be used in the treatment of mental health problems.
- The decision to take medication should be discussed thoroughly with a physician and monitored by a professional.

Group Therapy

- Group therapy is a form of support in which individuals with similar issues meet and share their experiences.
- This provides an excellent opportunity for building social support and developing coping skills.

Support from Specialized Medical Personnel

- In some cases, especially when dealing with severe mental disorders, support from medical personnel such as psychiatric nurses or occupational therapists is invaluable.

When to Seek Professional Help

- It's important to know when it's worth seeking help from professionals.
- This may be the moment when symptoms of mental health problems significantly impact daily functioning or when difficulties seem overwhelming.

Summary

In this chapter, we discussed the importance of specialist support in coping with mental and emotional problems. Professional help can be a crucial element in the process of healing and improving the quality of life. It's important to be aware of the available options and not hesitate to seek help when needed.

opportunities, and successes.

- Individuals with a positive perspective are more likely to make efforts, set goals, and work towards achieving them.

Negative Future Perspective

- A negative future perspective leads to feelings of hopelessness, lack of self-belief, and difficulty taking action.
- Individuals with a negative perspective may struggle with emotional issues such as depression or anxiety.

The Importance of Future Perspective in Therapy

- Therapists often work on changing their patients' future perspective, especially those suffering from mood disorders.
- Shifting from a negative perspective to a more positive one can be crucial for improving mental health.

How to Develop a Positive Future Perspective

- Goal Setting: Defining specific short-term and long-term goals helps focus on the future and motivates action.
- Building Coping Skills: Developing problem-solving skills and coping abilities can contribute to changing one's perspective.
- Cultivating Positive Thinking: Practicing positive thinking and eliminating negative beliefs can positively impact the future perspective.

Social Support and Future Perspective

- Family and friends can play a significant role in shaping our future perspective. Their support can reinforce self-belief.
- Social support can also be invaluable during challenging times and in maintaining a positive future perspective.

Summary

The future perspective has a tremendous impact on our emotional health. Adopting a positive perspective, setting goals, and developing coping skills can help build a healthy emotional life. Social support from loved ones and friends is a valuable source of assistance in the process of shifting to a more positive future perspective

Chapter 26: Hope as Motivation

Introduction:

In this chapter, we will discuss how hope can be a strong motivator and influence our actions and approach to life. We will understand why hope is such an important element in coping with emotional issues.

Hope as a Source of Motivation

- Hope is an emotion that fills us with optimism and faith in a positive future.
- This feeling motivates us to take action and strive to achieve our goals.

Hope and Focusing on the Future

- Hopeful individuals often have well-defined goals and dreams.
- Pursuing these goals provides them with motivation and satisfaction.

How to Cultivate Hope as Motivation

- Goal Setting: Defining specific short-term and long-term goals can fuel hope and motivation.
- Challenges as Opportunities: Instead of viewing difficulties as obstacles, hopeful people often see them as opportunities for learning and growth.
- Positive Thinking: Positive thinking and belief in a positive

future can be practiced and developed.

Hope in Therapy and Self-Help

- Therapists often work on strengthening hope in their patients, especially those with depression or other emotional problems.
- Changing a pessimistic outlook to a more hopeful one can be crucial for mental health.

Social Support and Hope

- Loved ones and friends can be significant sources of support and hope reinforcement.
- Supportive relationships can boost our self-belief and conviction that we can achieve positive outcomes.

Conclusion

Hope is a strong motivator that fills us with optimism and helps us achieve our goals. Cultivating hope as a source of motivation can aid in coping with emotional issues and pursuing a satisfying life. Social support from close individuals can be crucial in building and maintaining our hope.

Chapter 27: Social Support and Family

Introduction:

In this chapter, we will delve into the importance of social support and family in coping with emotional challenges. We'll explore how these relationships can serve as a vital source of strength, understanding, and encouragement during difficult times.

The Significance of Social Support

- Social support encompasses emotional, informational, and practical assistance from friends, acquaintances, and loved ones.
- It plays a pivotal role in emotional well-being and recovery from psychological issues.

Family as the Cornerstone of Support

- Family is often our primary source of support, offering unconditional love and care.
- Strong family bonds can provide a sense of belonging and safety, which is essential for mental health.

Types of Social Support

- Emotional Support: The empathetic listening and comfort provided by friends or family can help individuals feel understood and less alone in their struggles.
- Informational Support: Sharing knowledge and resources can empower individuals to make informed decisions about their mental health.
- Practical Support: Assistance with daily tasks or responsibilities can relieve stress and allow individuals to focus on self-care.

Cultivating Supportive Relationships

- Building strong relationships requires open communication, empathy, and trust.
- Honesty about your feelings and needs is crucial for receiving appropriate support.

Challenges in Seeking Support

- Stigma: The societal stigma surrounding mental health issues can deter individuals from seeking the support they need.
- Communication Barriers: Misunderstandings and miscommunication within relationships can impede effective support.

Family Dynamics and Support

- Family dynamics can significantly impact mental health.
- Dysfunctional family patterns may contribute to emotional challenges, but they can also be a source of healing and transformation.

Balancing Independence and Dependence

- While seeking support is essential, it's also crucial to maintain a sense of independence and self-reliance.
- Striking this balance can foster personal growth and resilience.

Conclusion

Social support, especially from family, is a cornerstone in coping with emotional challenges. Recognizing the types of support available and understanding how to cultivate healthy relationships can contribute significantly to emotional well-being. Despite challenges, seeking support and building strong connections remain vital for mental health.

Chapter 28: Personal Development

Introduction:

In this chapter, we will focus on the importance of personal development as a crucial strategy for coping with emotional problems. We will learn why continuous growth and self-improvement can bring significant benefits to mental health.

Personal Development

- Personal development is the deliberate process of striving to develop one's skills, knowledge, character traits, and attitudes.
- It is a long-term process that requires commitment and self-discipline.

The Importance of Personal Growth for Mental Health

- Working on oneself can help increase self-esteem and self-confidence.
- Developing skills to cope with stress and life difficulties can reduce the risk of emotional problems.

Goals of Personal Development

- Individuals working on personal development often set goals, such as improving interpersonal skills, achieving career success, or increasing self-awareness.
- Pursuing these goals can provide motivation and satisfaction.

Diverse Areas of Personal Growth

- Personal development can encompass various domains, such as learning, health, career, relationships, or spirituality.
- There are many actions that can be taken to achieve personal development goals.

Self-Discipline and Motivation

- Key factors for success in personal development are self-discipline and motivation.
- It is valuable to create an action plan and stick to it, even in the face of challenges.

Cultivating a Habit of Self-Improvement

- Consistent self-improvement practices can become a habit that accompanies us throughout our lives.
- It is worthwhile to invest time and effort in self-development because the benefits are enduring.

Summary

Working on personal development is an essential part of the process of coping with emotional problems. Understanding the significance of self-development, setting goals, and systematic practice can have positive effects on mental health. Striving for self-improvement and achieving personal goals can contribute to increased self-acceptance and better stress management.

The last chapter of this book is a tribute to every individual who has gone through emotional and psychological challenges. I understand that it may often feel like nobody truly comprehends the depth of your suffering or how difficult it is to function daily. However, you must know that you are incredibly important.

You are not alone in your emotional journey, even though it may sometimes seem that way. Many people care about you and want to help, regardless of where you find yourself on your path. That is precisely why this book was written - to provide support, guidance, and hope.

Understanding and accepting your emotional issues is the first step toward mental well-being. Even though this part of life can be challenging and burdensome at times, it is also your unique story that shapes your strength and uniqueness.

Now you know that there are various types of support and different methods to cope with emotional difficulties. You don't have to go through this alone. There is a society around you that will understand once you share your struggles with them. It's not shameful; it's not a weakness. It's human. It's courageous.

Ultimately, although it may be difficult to believe during the toughest times, there is hope. Hope for a brighter future where you can live life to the fullest, with joy, fulfillment, and love all around you. What you've been through can become a part of your story of overcoming and inspiring others.

Never forget that you matter. Your experiences matter. And even though the path may be challenging, you are capable of overcoming it. Each day is a new opportunity for health, finding meaning, and finding support.

Thank you for being a part of this book. Thank you for taking a step toward understanding and well-being. You are important, and you are loved. May this book be a source of hope and support for you when you need it. I believe in you.

www.ingramcontent.com/pod-product-compliance
Lightning Source LLC
Chambersburg PA
CBHW051357250726
48656CB00006B/2137